WOMEN LIKE ME COMMUNITY

LESSONS FROM MOM

JULIE FAIRHURST

ROCK STAR PUBLISHING

JULIE FAIRHURST

Paperback Edition: ISBN 978-1-990639-29-6
Interior & Cover Design by STOKE Publishing

Publisher:
Rock Star Publishing British Columbia, Canada Email: julie@changeyourpath.ca

CONTENTS

"Our mothers always remain the strangest,
craziest people we've ever met."

Marguerite Duras

COLLABORATIVE PUBLICATION

This is a collaborative publication, and you may notice variations in writing style from one piece to another. This is intentional, as it allows each writer to share their story in its authentic voice, preserving the uniqueness of their contribution.

We believe their raw and genuine perspectives bring a richness to this collection that polished writing alone cannot capture. Each story reflects the individual journey and truth of the writer, which we honor and celebrate.

Some of these women are "first-time authors, not professional writers, but they have poured their hearts and experiences into these pages.

Every woman participating in the Women Like Me program shares a common purpose: "If my story can help even one person, then sharing it is truly worthwhile.

"My mother... she is beautiful, softened at the edges and tempered
with a spine of steel.
I want to grow old and be like her."

Jodi Picoult

DISCLOSURE

Dear Beautiful Reader,

Before you dive into the powerful, soul-stirring stories that make up the Women Like Me book series, I want to offer you a gentle heads-up—heart to heart.

These pages are rich with truth, courage, and the kind of resilience that rises from the ashes of real-life struggle. But as inspiring as these stories are, they're not a replacement for professional medical, psychological, or therapeutic support. These aren't prescriptions, they're lived experiences—raw, honest, and beautifully human.

And sometimes? They hit deep.

If you find yourself feeling overwhelmed or triggered as you read, please don't carry it alone. Reach out. Talk to someone you trust—a friend, a counselor, a therapist. Let someone hold space for you while you process. Asking for support is not weakness—it's wisdom, it's strength, and it's one of the bravest things you'll ever do.

This journey isn't about doing it all on your own. It's about walking together—with grace, grit, and the full-hearted knowing that healing is possible.

So go ahead—flip these pages. Let the words meet you where you are. Let the voices of these incredible women remind you that your story matters, your voice is valid, and your strength is already within you, just waiting to be remembered.

Now, let's begin—side by side—with courage, compassion, and a whole lot of heart.

With love and belief in you,

Julie Fairhurst

Founder, Women Like Me

"When your mother asks, "Do you want a piece of advice?" it's a mere formality. It doesn't matter if you answer yes or no.
You're going to get it anyway."

Erma Bombeck

INTRODUCTION

LESSONS FROM MOM

The title says it all, doesn't it?

Every one of us carries stories etched into our hearts by the women who raised us—some of those lessons shine with love, strength, and stability. Others? They're bruised with misunderstanding, silence, or survival.

But here's the deeper truth—those lessons, whether blessings or burdens, were passed down through a long line of women doing the best they could with what they had. Your mother learned from her mother, and she from hers. The thread winds through generations, stitched with inherited beliefs, pain unspoken, and the quiet hope that maybe, just maybe, things could be different.

And now? Now it's our turn.

We are the generation with the power to wake up. To break the chain. To unlearn what no longer serves us, or our children. We are the cycle shifters, the generational pattern disruptors. If we don't rise in awareness and choose differently, we'll unknowingly hand those same tired teachings down to the next generation like an unwanted heirloom.

But we don't have to.

We can choose to do it differently. We can plant seeds of healing, self-worth, emotional safety, and true connection. We can teach our children to stand tall in their truth, not shrink to fit the shape of our wounds.

And for those of you who were gifted with lessons rooted in love, compassion, and wisdom, what a treasure. You are the living proof of what's possible when generations pass along grounding, not grief. That solid foundation is a gift you now get to expand, evolve, and share with those who come next.

We say it often, but let's mean it here: "When we know better, we do better."

And our mothers? They may not have known. They may not have had the luxury of knowledge, time, safety, or support. They did what they could, and sometimes that wasn't enough. But instead of placing blame, we place understanding. And from that understanding, we rise.

I'm so grateful for us, this generation of brave women willing to ask the hard questions and do the deeper work. I see it in our daughters. I see it in our sons. I see it in the strength rising in our grandchildren. They are already rewriting the story, and it's a beautiful thing to witness.

This is the gift of healing: it doesn't stop with us. It ripples through our families and into the future.

And really, isn't that the most powerful legacy of all?

IN **LESSONS FROM MOM**, 13 courageous women open their

hearts and share powerful glimpses into the lives of their mothers, their triumphs, their struggles, and the life lessons that shaped them.

Some stories will make you laugh; others might make you cry, but every single one will remind you of the profound impact a mother's legacy can leave.

So, settle in, open your heart, and enjoy this book. It was written with love, truth, and a whole lot of soul.

Julie Fairhurst

Founder of Women like Me

"All that I am or ever hope to be, I owe to my angel mother."

Abraham Lincoln

PART 1

LESSONS FROM MOM

1

THE INHERITANCE OF LESSONS

WHAT WE LEARN FROM OUR MOTHERS, WHAT WE SHOULD PASS ON, AND WHAT WE MUST LAY TO REST.

We learn how to live long before we ever speak.

We watch. We mimic. We absorb.

And for most of us, our mothers were our first mirrors, reflecting back to us not just what was said, but what was shown.

From our mothers, we inherited a legacy, not of money or medals, but of behaviors, beliefs, and boundaries (or lack thereof). Some of these are the blueprints for strength, resilience, and love. Others are burdens too heavy to carry into the next generation.

So, let's talk about both—the radiant truths and the quiet wounds—and let's decide together which lessons we pass on like heirlooms and which ones we bury with grace.

The Positive Lessons Worth Passing On

1. Love that defies logic

Many of us witnessed the kind of love that had no limits. Late nights. Empty stomachs. Silent sacrifices. A mother's love taught us what devotion looks like in action—and it's a love we often pour into our own children.

2. Resilience wrapped in routine.

Even when she was breaking inside, she made the lunches. Paid the bills. Showed up. Her strength wasn't always loud, but it was steady. We saw that courage doesn't always wear armor. Sometimes it wears aprons, sweatpants, and a tired smile.

3. Resourcefulness in scarcity.

Some mothers could make miracles out of nothing. A feast from scraps. A holiday from thin air. They showed us how to stretch a dollar, improvise joy, and find light when the electricity was out in every sense of the word.

These are the lessons to keep. To pass. To live out loud.

The Negative Lessons We Must Stop Handing Down

1. Martyrdom as motherhood.

We were taught that to be good mothers, we must be selfless. She didn't buy the dress. She skipped the doctor's appointment. She abandoned her dreams at the altar of "for the kids." We admired it. We even repeated it. But it's time to retire that narrative. Because being a martyr doesn't breed heroes. It breeds generations of women who believe their worth is tied to how much they can suffer silently.

2. Silence over self-expression.

"Don't make a scene."

"Don't rock the boat."

"Just smile."

Too many girls learned early that keeping the peace was more important than keeping your voice. That compliance was currency. And that emotional expression made you "too much." It's time to rewrite that script. We need daughters who speak up, who cry without shame, and who never apologize for taking up space.

3. Dreams are for later... or never.

We watched our mothers postpone their passions until the kids were grown, the house was clean, or the husband gave permission. Sometimes "later" never came. And whether she meant to or not, she taught us: your dreams are negotiable. Disposable. Optional.

But they're not. They're sacred. They're the fire in our bellies. And they deserve to be fed.

Why Being Positively "Selfish" Is the Boldest Legacy You Can Leave

Let's reclaim that word, selfish, because somewhere along the line, it was twisted into something shameful. But what if selfish means self-honoring?

What if it means showing your kids that you are a person, not a servant?

What if the most powerful thing we can do for our daughters and sons is to show them a woman who dreams and dares, who says no when needed, and who invests in herself, not just her family?

Because when children see their mother light up doing something she loves, they learn that joy is not indulgent, it's essential.

When they watch her say no to what drains her, and yes to what energizes her, they learn how to honor their own boundaries.

When they see her fall in love with life again at 40, or 50, or 75, they know it's never too late to begin again.

And our girls? They grow up believing they matter. Not just as helpers or healers or hustlers, but as humans.

A Final Note to Every Mother Reading This

You are not just raising a child.

You are raising a future adult who will one day raise, lead, create, or care for others.

So don't just teach them to survive.

Teach them to thrive.

Be the woman who breaks the pattern.

Be the mother who becomes her own hero.

And show your children, by example, that every chapter of life is still yours to write.

Even the one where you choose you.

Julie Fairhurst

"Despite the challenges my mother faced, despite the limitations placed on her as a woman, she taught me that true strength is not about the roles you are given, but how you rise above them."

Hagir Elsheikh

2

SHERON CHISHOLM

"Mother's love is peace. It need not be acquired, it need not be deserved."
Erich Fromm

My wonderful mom: her life was too short, but she accomplished so much.

Mom was always quiet, and gentle and had a "special" sweetness about her that attracted most children and adults. She inspired people to smile just by being near her! These features also kept our family together and running smoothly.

She arranged our outings such as picnics with friends and vacations. Participating in her children's activities was important to her, and she was consistent in being involved in parent-teacher functions and was president of this group.

At the same time, she gave space for developing independence and becoming the true me.

She taught me that being involved in the lives of your children is an important way to teach them how much you love them. Girl Scouts was my interest throughout my school days and my mother came to meetings, went camping with us, and helped me earn badges.

My sister was too young for my group, so my mother started a group for girls her age. She taught compassion and unselfishness in many ways. She gave up her own time to play games with us, sew clothes for us, cook for us, and make sure we had everything we needed.

Mom taught vacation Bible School, Sunday School, and was a member of the Alter Guild. She made sure we prayed before meals and bedtime. She truly was a saint of God's.

I had never thought of her this way until our minister made the comment at her funeral. And it made me cry. She was a servant to everyone she met, showing them love and acceptance with humility.

She wasn't perfect, but we are not expected to be!

"A daughter without her mother is a woman broken. It is a loss that turns to arthritis and settles deep into her bones."

Kristin Hannah

3

GIFT OKIH

"Men always want to be a woman's first love; women like to be a man's last romance."
Oscar Wilde

Love, Self, and Everything in Between

"Don't get carried away with love." Several teenagers and young female adults have heard the previous statement. Even if not in the same terms, the message has been passed on to them. If you haven't heard the opening statement, I'm reiterating it.

A mom once said it to me, not because love isn't beautiful, but because it shouldn't be the sole focus of teenage life. You should learn to live fully, explore life, and enjoy all its beauties.

We know how the classic story goes: A girl meets a boy, feels butter-flies, and sometimes gets absorbed in her feelings, losing sight of everything else. While it's okay to love, crush, and like, it's not worth losing yourself over.

Before you throw caution to the wind, take a minute and ask yourself if you've truly discovered who you are. What makes you tick? What's the essence of your being? What gladdens your core? What's your purpose? It's important to embark on a journey of self-discovery at an early stage.

Make your life about you before you shift focus. There's a lot to learn in life that will open your eyes to surprising realities. Your first love may not be the one.

Guys love with logic. They're calculative and make decisions uninfluenced by emotions. But women are always quick to bend to the whims of their emotions, throwing all caution away. So, while most males are emotionally stoic, females wear their hearts on their sleeves.

You might have been like that once and made a few mistakes, but it's never too late to get your life back on track. If you're young and haven't worn these shoes, be careful. Don't fall in love with reckless abandon. You've got to learn to balance your emotions. It's okay to have fun, but don't get carried away and make wrong decisions.

Building emotional intelligence will enable you to prioritize your well-being and sanity so you'll know when to walk away. It's annoying when younger girls date older men or guys who exploit their naivety and cross boundaries. But if you know what suits you, selecting a partner whose values align with yours will be easy.

One that will respect your decisions and boundaries while upholding your standards. You don't have to relinquish your identity to keep a man. Instead, just be you. You're worthy of love, respect, and honor. Live your life right and thrive on all fronts. Don't downplay yourself to sustain a budding feeling. If the dynamics feel like you have to be subordinate to boost your partner's ego, sit back and rethink.

A relationship shouldn't make you self-isolate, nor should your partner be the center of your world. Indulge in all your favorite activities, develop academically, groom your friendships, learn skills, and gain work experience. This way, you can maintain individuality and evade codependency.

As you grow on all fronts, also practice self-care. Have regular spa days, book nail and hair appointments, and read books to develop your mind. Plan and strategize your life from an early stage.

Your teenage years are the time to begin nursing and feeding your ambitions. Discover your goals and write them down. Ensure your goals are SMART (Specific, Measurable, Achievable, Realistic, and Time-bound). Decide on specific steps to help you achieve your goals, especially your financial ones.

You must also develop a sense of self-worth; it'll help you out yourself first in all circumstances.

Interestingly, this comes from knowing who you are. Be cold and confident in your personality. If it means writing powerful statements about yourself on post it notes and saying them daily, do it.

You, my dear, are a sensual lady. You're phenomenal, beautiful, strong, and powerful. Never let anyone make you cower or doubt your worth. Love is special, but so are you! I hope this piece impacts someone out there.

With love,

Gift Okih.

"The most remarkable thing about my mother is that for thirty years she served the family nothing but leftovers. The original meal has never been found."

Calvin Trillin

4

THERESA WAUGH

**"Love begins at home, and it is not how much wedo…
but how much love we put in that action."**
Mother Teresa

For years, I felt like I was drowning. As the mother of seven adult children, my life revolved around solving their problems, offering advice, and cushioning their falls. I was the go-to person for everything, from financial woes to relationship dramas.

My days were a whirlwind of phone calls, errands, and sleepless nights spent worrying. The exhaustion was all-consuming, the stress relentless. I loved my children fiercely, but I was losing myself in the process.

My Breaking Point

The turning point came during a particularly difficult week. I was juggling multiple crises – one child struggling with a job loss, another facing a health scare, and a third dealing with relationship issues. I felt completely overwhelmed, stretched thin, and utterly depleted.

One evening, as I sat alone in my living room, tears streaming down my face, I had a profound realization: I couldn't keep doing this. I was so focused on fixing everyone else's lives that I had neglected my own.

It wasn't that I stopped caring, but I understood I was enabling them and harming myself. I had to learn to let go and allow them to navigate their own paths, even if it meant making mistakes along the way. I started to understand that my anxiety about their lives was my problem, not theirs.

My Self-Care and Independence

I made a conscious decision to shift my focus inward. Self-care, which had always seemed like a luxury, became a necessity. I started prioritizing my own needs and well-being.

I began with small steps: taking daily walks, reading books, and practicing mindfulness. I rediscovered hobbies I had long abandoned, like painting and gardening. I started saying 'no' to requests that drained my energy and 'yes' to activities that nourished my soul.

I communicated my new boundaries to my children. I explained that while I would always be there for them emotionally, I could no longer be their default problem-solver. It wasn't easy.

There were moments of resistance, frustration, and even anger. But I stood my ground, gently reminding them that I believed in their ability to handle their own lives.

I found that focusing on gratitude helped me appreciate the good things in my life, despite the challenges. A good night's sleep had an amazing impact on my well-being. I began to feel more rested and energized, and I was better able to cope with stress.

Rediscovering old hobbies filled my life with joy and purpose. I felt more creative, more engaged, and more alive.

These four core self-care changes were life changing for me and my family.

- Setting Boundaries
- Practicing Gratitude
- Prioritizing Sleep
- Nurturing Hobbies

The Ripple Effect

As I changed, so did my relationships with my children. They started to step up and take more responsibility for their own choices. They learned to rely on their own resourcefulness and resilience. They discovered their own strength and independence. The dynamic shifted from one of dependence to one of mutual respect and support.

One of my children recently said to me, 'Mom, I used to think you had all the answers. Now I realize that you were just holding my hand while I found them myself.' That statement filled me with immense pride and gratitude. I had finally succeeded in empowering my children to become the best versions of themselves.

I learned that true love isn't about fixing someone else's problems; it's about supporting their growth and believing in their ability to thrive.

I now approach life with a sense of peace and contentment that I never thought possible. I have energy, pursue my interests, and am a better mother than I ever was before.

Words of Encouragement

My journey from exhaustion to empowerment has taught me invaluable lessons about self-care, boundaries, and the transformative power of letting go.

If you're a caregiver feeling overwhelmed and depleted, please know that you're not alone. It's okay to prioritize your own needs.

It's okay to set boundaries. It's okay to say 'no.' In fact, it's essential.

By taking care of yourself, you'll not only improve your own well-being but also empower your loved ones to take responsibility for their own lives.

Remember, you can't pour from an empty cup. Fill your cup first, and then you'll have the energy and strength to support others from a place of abundance and love.

"Mothers and their children are in a category
all their own.
There's no bond so strong in the entire world.
No love so instantaneous and forgiving."

Gail Tsukiyama

5

TAMMIE TRITES

"I wasn't born to carry the pain — I was born to end it. In choosing healing, I broke the chains my ancestors never could, and built a future my children never have to escape from. I am the rewriter of my bloodline."
Tammie Trites

Breaking the Chains: My Story of Generational Healing.

I was born into chaos. My earliest memories are a blur of shouting voices, slammed doors, and the overwhelming weight of silence that followed the storms. Love in my house was something we all craved but rarely received.

Affection came with conditions, and sometimes, not at all. My parents, caught in the grip of their own unresolved pain, passed it down like an unwanted heirloom. They didn't mean to, but trauma has a way of trickling down, generation after generation, unless someone is brave enough to stop it.

My childhood was filled with contradictions. Laughter lived right next to fear. I could be playing with my friends one moment and hiding under the bed the next, trying to make myself invisible.

Alcohol flowed freely in our home. The adults stumbled through life, numbing their own childhood wounds, while we children watched, learned, and absorbed.

Anger was the default language, and silence was how we coped.

There were nights I'd lie awake, praying to a God I didn't fully understand, begging him to make it stop, the yelling, the hitting, the drinking, the crying. I didn't have the words back then, but I knew something wasn't right.

I knew that love wasn't supposed to feel like fear.

I used to dream about running away, but even as a child, I understood that no matter how far I ran, I'd carry those wounds with me.

The pain didn't stop when I became a teenager. If anything, it intensified. I started to feel like I was drowning in everything I didn't understand. I watched my friends live what looked like normal lives.

Their parents hugged them, showed up to school events, remembered birthdays. I wanted that so badly. But in my house, we were just trying to survive the day.

By the time I became an adult, I had a choice to make. I could repeat the cycle, after all, it was all I knew, or I could break it. But breaking the cycle isn't as simple as just wanting to do better. It means facing the very things you tried to bury. It means dragging old wounds into the light, examining them, healing them even when it hurts like hell.

The biggest shift came when I became a mother. Holding my first child in my arms, I knew instantly: this ends with me. She was perfect, untouched by the pain I had carried for so long. I made a silent promise right then and there, that I would never let her feel the kind of fear I knew all too well. That I would give her what I had always longed for: safety, stability, love without conditions.

It wasn't easy. Healing is not linear. Some days, I'd lose my temper and hear my mother's voice in my own. I'd freeze in horror, realizing how easily the past could sneak back in.

But I learned to pause. To breathe. To apologize, something I had never once heard growing up.

I taught my daughters that emotions were not something to be ashamed of. That crying was okay. That asking for help was strong. That love was not earned, but it was given freely.

Over the years, I read books. I prayed. I cried rivers. I had to unlearn everything I thought I knew about parenting, about love, about myself. I looked back at my childhood, not to assign blame, but to understand.

My parents had been wounded, too. They were raised in homes where survival came first, where no one had the tools to love properly. They weren't monsters. They were broken. And for the first time, I felt compassion for them, not anger.

Still, I chose a different path. I built a home filled with laughter, softness, and honesty.

My daughters grew up knowing they were cherished. They saw me struggle, but they also saw me fight. They saw resilience, not rage. They learned that breaking doesn't mean you're weak, it means you're human.

One of the proudest moments of my life was when my oldest daughter told me, "You gave us the life you never had." She had no idea the depth of that truth. Every meal we shared, every bedtime story, every I love you; those were all rebellions against the past. Every hug was a battle won. Every safe night's sleep was a victory.

The dysfunction didn't disappear overnight. Sometimes it creeps back in unexpected ways. A triggered memory. A nightmare. A hard day that makes me feel twelve years old again. But the difference now is, I don't let it take over.

I name it. I sit with it. I remind myself that I am not that scared little girl anymore. I am a grown woman who chose to rewrite the story.

Breaking generational trauma doesn't mean pretending it never happened. It means honoring the past, while refusing to let it define the future. It means loving harder, even when you don't know how. It means choosing forgiveness, not because they deserve it, but because you deserve peace.

If you had told me when I was ten years old that I would grow up to raise a family full of laughter and light, I wouldn't have believed you. But here I am.

The cycle is broken. My daughters are free. And so am I.

"God could not be everywhere,
and therefore he made mothers."

David C. Gross

6

THERESA CAMPBELL

"You count the hours you could have spent with your mother, it's a lifetime in itself."
Mitch Albom

A Letter to My Mother

Dear mother,

Although you have passed from this earth, I think of you often.

For better and for worse, you have taught me many lessons, some intentionally and others unintentionally. I have felt both love and anger toward you.

I carry the lessons I have learned from you and over the years I have learned to discern which lessons came from love and which lessons came from fear. I now acknowledge that I may have passed on some good and bad lessons on to my own children and that is why I am learning to understand those lessons.

I am grateful for the lessons that originated in love.

You taught me empathy and compassion for others. I strived to be a helper and a healer. I watched you as a child when you listened intently to the needs of others and comforted them.

You gave your time and your energy without question. No matter how tired you were feeling at the time, you pushed yourself to help others, particularly the people who were vulnerable, challenged in some way.

On the other hand, your empathy and compassion were stretched to the limit. You gave above and beyond what a human being should be required to give. I was influenced by that lesson and became a person who feels compelled to give.

As a result, I feel exhausted and drained. It took years before I could recognize this. You taught this lesson unintentionally. I honour your commitment to helping others. I now understand the importance of balance, boundaries and self care. I wish I could have helped you.

At the time, I was just a child and could do nothing but observe and try to make you happy. I am grateful for another good lesson. You taught me to work hard and to always give my best. If a job is worth doing, it's worth doing well.

That was your attitude. If the job required a skill set you didn't have, you quickly acquired the skills. I admired your determination in that regard. You did not shy away from a challenge and that lesson stuck with me.

On the other hand, you would often criticize yourself for not being good enough. I observed your negative self criticism and was puzzled by it. I was a child and could not offer you advice or offer a better perspective. I simply listened and felt bad for you, helpless and unsure of what to say or do.

As a young adult, I carried a voice of self criticism. This voice came from fear, not love and it was not helpful.

I now understand that you struggled with self doubt and the need for validation. You needed to recognize that your feelings toward yourself were self sabotaging and totally unnecessary. You did not recognize it. I am grateful for your lessons regarding integrity.

You taught me to be mindful of my choices. Every choice has a consequence, and that consequence should not compromise your integrity.

When we are young, there is an urge for us to challenge the rules and do what we choose to do. However, there are a variety of factors influencing us at this time.

For example, peer pressure and unstable hormones may push us in a risky direction. You taught me to think for myself and be mindful of possible outcomes. I did the best I could under the circumstances.

On the other hand, being a people pleaser, I struggled at the crossroads from teenager to young adult. I wanted to please you and make you proud but felt enormous pressure.

I had some experience as a young athlete trying to be disciplined and gain recognition, accolades, and success. The pressure was too much. I began feeling this way again in young adulthood.

The pressure seemed overwhelming, but I continued to present myself confidently and gracefully. It was exhausting. It felt like pretending all the time.

Yes, I was holding back. I had more to give, but I was stuck. Now, I am aware of my need to please people, and I try to be realistic. It's not my job to please everyone. We don't need to put pressure on ourselves to do amazing things. We can do amazing without pressure.

I am grateful for the lesson of faith in yourself and others. Most of the time you saw the best in others, and I believe you tried to be a beacon of light for others in spite of your struggles with self worth.

You dedicated your life to raising a family and then spent years volunteering and advocating for others who needed to be appreciated and accepted in their communities. You understood the importance of standing up for justice and fairness for all.

We all are deserving of love. I wish you could have appreciated yourself more because clearly you cared more for others than you did for yourself. I remember seeing you alone, on your bed, your porthole to the afterlife as you lay dying. I had no words other than, I love you.

Mother, I hope you are at peace and truly understand how much you are loved. I think that being a mother is an extremely important job, and we need to love ourselves and truly be comfortable with who we are and who we wish to become so that we may influence our children in the best possible way.

And this is the most important lesson I learned from you.

Thank you. Your daughter, Tess

"There's nothing like your mother's sympathetic voice to make you want to burst into tears."

Sophie Kinsella

7

JODI STURGILL

Sometimes, mothers say and do things that seem like they don't want their kids... but when you look more closely, you realize that they're doing those kids a favor. They're just trying to give them a better life."
Jodi Picoult

Twenty-Eight Years Ago

I have four children who are grown up now. I was a single parent part of the time when they were younger.

We were living in Parksville on Vancouver Island, in British Columbia. This is where all my children grew up.

When my youngest child, Brad was about seven years old, he went to the store with his older brother and came back with some candy.

He told me he didn't pay for it! So, I made him go back to the store and return it and say sorry to the store employee.

It was a good lesson for him, and he never did it again. He always made sure he had money to buy something, or he wouldn't take it.

I believe it is important when our children do something we know is wrong, we make them deal with the consequences of their actions. If we don't how will they ever learn right from wrong.

"Even as a small child, I understood that woman had secrets, and that some of these were only to be told to daughters. In this way we were bound together for eternity."

Alice Hoffman

8

LISA ELLIS

"Blessed is a mother that would give up part of her soul for her children's happiness."
Shannon L. Alder

I wrote this in honour of my Mom who went to be with the Lord on July 11, 2022, after a short battle of Lung Cancer

Hi Mom, how are you doing up there? I hope you are doing okay! Is it beautiful in Heaven like they say? I hope your pain is gone and you can breathe better now?!

You always had a Kleenex in your pocket, candy in your purse and every date marked on the calendar. You knew every celebration, everyone's birthday, every appointment.

You knew it all and you never forgot anyone. You always gave that reminder that everyone needs, whether it be, "did you go for your sticker yet? Don't forget you have your appointment coming up, how is work going?"

It's those little things that I miss the most. Just knowing that you were always looking out for us.

Like most every time I would go for a visit, which was often, you would say, "Hey Lisa, do you want this moose for your hair? Or do you need a new calendar? Or I bought this shampoo and conditioner, and I don't like it, so you can have it. Do you need some more plastic containers?"

I loved going to bingo with Mom. She would have so many bingo cards in front of her and I would just have my two sheets I never knew how she could play so many cards at once. She would dob her numbers and still have time to check mine. Bingo was always something fun and exciting that I looked forward to with Mom.

Your graceful walk, your loving touch, your sweet voice, your pleasant smile, your soft skin, the sparkle in your eyes and Christmas because it was your favourite holiday.

These are just some of the things that come to my mind when I think about you.

To me, you were a Mother, a Nana to my Children and a great Nana to my Grandchildren, but most of all, you were my comforter, my teacher, my motivator. You were the person who knew it all You were my go-to person in any situation.

You were my world and now you are my Angel.

You have taught me the most valuable things in life (patience, love, kindness, manners and respect, strength and how to pray). You are by far, the strongest, most patient person I knew, and you make me proud.

Despite your battles, you were strong and still so concerned about everyone else. You didn't want us to worry about you. You are a true fighter, a true Angel. No wonder God wanted you for himself.

Mom, I am sorry you were sick, and I wish I could have changed the outcome.

I wrote you a letter the same day that you spoke to your Oncologist through phone consultation. It was the day you found out that your Cancer was Stage 4. I remember everything about that call.

How scared I felt for you, knowing you had to listen as she was telling you what was happening to your body, scared for myself, not knowing what was being said, heart broken of the possibility of losing you and terrified to answer your call for fear of receiving bad news.

Then the call came, and I answered. I still remember every word you said, like a bullet through my heart. "Well honey, there is no cure," you said. "They can't cure it. All they can do is stabilize it with radiation and chemotherapy to prolong my life. They said it's already stage 4, so it's too late. They don't know exactly how long I have."

This was not the news I was expecting at all. I could not believe it.

I have learned a lot going through this Cancer journey with you. Learning that there will never be a right time is just one, not having enough time, is another. I have learned to accept things for what they are, no matter how hard it may seem because you see, I never accepted the fact that you were going to die because I didn't want you to die.

I was in denial and when the thought came to my mind, I just kept pushing it away.

Mom, it's weird and hard to explain because I was sad and upset of the thought of losing you, but a part of me still thought I wasn't going to. I kept having hope which is another thing I was taught, despite what the tests showed or what the Doctor's said.

You have taught me to smile when I feel like all I want to do is cry, you have taught me to appreciate life and the time that you have. You have taught me how to be strong when I wanted to be weak. You taught me to pray and pray some more, even when it feels like all hope is gone.

There were many times I felt like prayer was all I had.

You have taught me patience and unconditional love.

Mom, losing you was the worse thing that has ever happened to me and watching you die, was even harder. Then Lori was diagnosed with Cancer of the Pancreas and died just eight months after you.

Jaiden and I were there to comfort her, the same way that she was there with us to comfort you. It was crazy Mom, to lose my sister just eight months after losing you. It was hard.

Did you see Lori Mom? Are you guys together again? I am going to hold the comfort in my heart that you are both reunited.

It's different living my life without you. Like there are still times I wish I could call you on the phone or visit you and have coffee together. Maybe someday Mom.

Happy Mother's Day in Heaven Mom.

Thank you for giving me the gift of life and teaching me so many things. I owe it all to you.

And God, please take good care of my Mom and love her the way I do! Please wrap your loving arms around her and tell her it's a hug from her daughter.

To all the readers who are still blessed with having their Mom, please hold her tight and cherish her for you never know how much time you have left and the loss of a Mother is one of the greatest losses you'll ever experience!

And for those who have lost their Mom, I feel your pain.

The way I look at it, I didn't loose a Mom, I gained an Angel who looks down on me everyday with her protection and guidance. She might not be in sight, but she will always be in my heart.

Your Mom is always with you

"Mothers were the only ones you could depend on to tell the whole, unvarnished truth."

Margaret Dilloway

9

CATHERINE CHAPMAN-KING

"Do the best you can until you know better. Then when you know better, do better."
Maya Angelou

A Mother's Love and Lessons That Last a Lifetime

April 1st 1977, when I was just three years old, my brother Matt and I were adopted by the Chapmans. Terry, our new father, and Carole Ann our new mother. At the time, I had no idea how profoundly being adopted would shape the rest of my life.

Looking back now, with the clarity of 20/20 hindsight, I see it for what it truly was a blessing beyond measure and I'm so deeply grateful.

My mother Carole was the embodiment of love, grace, and strength. A Christian woman through and through, and it showed in everything she did.

Every action, every word, every meal...it was laced with her pure intention and care. She didn't just raise us children; she nurtured our hearts, guided our souls, and she led by example.

I tried my best to mirror that with my own children.

My brother Matt and I were adopted because my mother Carole had suffered numerous miscarriages, and she was told by doctors that she wouldn't be able to carry a pregnancy to term.

That heartbreaking journey led her to us, and though we weren't born of her body, we were born straight into her heart.

She never made us feel anything less than completely and unconditionally her and my fathers' children...And then, as life would have it, when she was 40 years old just nine years before she passed away, she miraculously became pregnant with our little brother Peter.

I call him Peteski, he's only recently admitted he hates that nick name but tolerates it because I'm his sis. Peteski was the blessing she had once thought impossible.

Tragically, not long after having Peter, she was diagnosed with cancer. He was only eight years old when she passed away.

We grew up in the city, in a lovely neighborhood that somehow managed to feel like a little patch of our own paradise, especially because of my mother's garden. It wasn't just a garden; it was a world of its own.

From rhubarb to watermelon to the pumpkins that lit up our Halloween nights, she really grew it all including fresh herbs. Nearly everything we ate came from that soil in my Mum's garden, tended by her with love. The only exception was the meat.

Even our morning orange juice came freshly squeezed oranges one by one by my mother, one glass per child. At the time, I didn't understand the rarity or the gift of that. I just thought it was normal; I thought that every child had a family like this and live like this. But now, I see how extraordinary it was. I'm so grateful.

I remember friends telling me they grew up on Kraft Dinner and hot dogs, never having a home cooked meal, never going to a cottage or experiencing camp. And there I was, living what felt like a fairy tale in comparison.

We had a cottage on Lake Couchiching, not far from Casino Rama. Every season brought its own magic, so many great memories from there growing up. It was on that lake that I got my bronze medallion testing so that I could be a lifeguard.

In the fall, the cottages around us would gather to help each other with repairs, and I'd be in the coffee truck, handing out tea, cookies, and warm smiles.

In the winter, I'd run around in snowshoes so I wouldn't sink into the deep snow and boy was there a lot of deep snow up North. I would help tap the trees for maple syrup, what we called "Chapman's Liquid Gold." My father Terry would cook up gold. Yummy.

My mother taught us not just how to live, but how to live well with grace, purpose, and always with love. She made our Halloween costumes by hand, so intricate, beautiful creations that could rival store-bought ones any day hands down. She even sewed matching sundresses for her and me when I was little.

I remember her walking with such poise and dignity, always reminding me to act, speak, and carry myself like a young lady.

While my father believed in teaching us how to "dance with the devil" and defend ourselves in a rough world, my mother believed in walking away from conflict, turning the other cheek, and preserving one's grace. I learned a lot of really valuable life lessons from the both of them.

She was the kind of mother who never raised her voice, never swore, never hit. She parented with such a gentleness and integrity. And when it came to safety, she was unmatched. "Safety first," she'd always say—whether it was riding our BMX bikes with embarrassing hockey helmets (thank God, I wore mine the day I crashed face-first into a parked car showing off to my brother) or taking my first solo ride on the Toronto Transit Commission. She made sure I sat at the front near the driver, just so I'd be safe.

I was a tomboy, wild and free, always testing boundaries. And yet, my Mum never tried to tame me, she just guided me.

Her cooking was legendary—especially her apple crisp and the award-winning salads with fruits, seeds, and a burst of color that made every plate feel like art. Meals were never just food. They were nourishment for the body and the soul, meals that you could present to a king or queen most definitely.

More than anything else, my mother taught me what it meant to love. Not just to feel it, but to show it in how we treat others, how we care for our families, how we show up in the world.

She taught me patience, compassion, and communication. She taught me to lead with love, no matter the situation. When she was dying, she wasn't worried about herself. She was worried about everyone else. That's who she was so selfless, strong, radiant to her final breath.

She passed at the age of 49. At the time, that seemed old to me, but I'm now 51, and I realize how young she really was. It rattles me to think she didn't get to see her grandchildren grow, didn't get the full measure of life in certain ways... and yet, she lives on in me, my brothers Matt and Petski.

She still lives in every value I carry; in every loving choice I make. It took me a long time to fully grasp how lucky I was. But now I know. And, there's not a day that goes by that I do not think a higher power for being adopted.

I know she's still watching, still guiding and hopefully still proud of me. You know, if every child had a mother like mine, the world would be a gentler place.

So, here's to my mother, Carole Ann Chapman, A PHENOMENAL woman whose love shaped our family, myself, my brothers and generations to follow.

Her legacy is stitched into the very fabric of who I am.

"Mom had the kind of love for her
that you could feel,
like it was part of the atmosphere"

Peter Abrahams

10

PATTERS

"As parents, one of the most valuable things we can instill in our children is that they matter, they are special, and they are here on this earth for a special purpose."

The Mom Psychologist

Mom's life lessons.... there are so many that I could write a book on them! Yet this child of hers had a challenge learning them all! However, the most precious lesson my Mom taught me was the gifted lesson of ACCEPTANCE.

When I was born, Mom accepted her little baby girl despite me being born with Spina Bifida, a neural tube defect and the onslaught of the unknowns she would face along the way.

Lesson 1 - Keep Moving!

Before the age of five, and after several surgeries, mom taught me how to move my legs with endless therapeutic exercises, then crawl, stand up, fall down, stand up again, find my balance, take a few steps and then finally walk unaided!

With these learned lessons I was able to get around independently and attend school like all the other five-year-old children!

Lesson 2 - Repeat and Keep Moving Forward!

I endured many more surgeries during my childhood and after each of them I would have to learn how to walk with and without the use of mobility aids, and there was mom repeating these lessons and retraining me repeatedly all over again!

These repeated lessons gave me the ability to do so many things! I was able to be active and play with other children, I learned how to do somersaults and headstands, go camping and do many other fun activities with my family.

Lesson 3 - Stay Focused and Remember What You Have Accomplished!

With these previous learned lessons I succeeded yet it was increasingly becoming hard for me mentally to accept the way my body was and how it would fail me at times to do what the average person could do that I couldn't.

When I was in my late teens, life became so overwhelming that I lost focus on these lessons. I struggled to accept the things that I couldn't physically do as well as not being accepted by my peers. I felt like life didn't seem to matter anymore and I became very depressed to the point that I attempted suicide.

Luckily, my Dad stopped me in the nick of time and although I wanted to leave this world, I'm so thankful that I didn't.

My Mom had wrapped me in her arms once again and told me to keep moving forward no matter what may happen in life, that I was a worthy, capable, and beautiful girl and I hold a special purpose in this world. She sat me down and reminded me of all the things that I had accomplished so far and of all the things that I could still accomplish in the future. Focusing on what I couldn't do impacted my ability to accept me, for me!

I realized that shifting my focus will allow me to accept who I am and what I could do versus what I couldn't do which was imperative to move forward!

Lesson 4 - Learn Acceptance!

Mom continued to provide her love and supportive encouragement as I made my way through the many obstacles that life presented. Although my struggles continued into adulthood, my outlook was different as I learned to love who I was and for the things that I had accomplished. I finally accepted me for me and saw a promising future!

The lessons Mom taught me made me into the woman I am today and has driven me to accomplish amazing things throughout my 62 years of life, far exceeding my life expectancy of 12 years old!

I learned to walk (although now I use a wheelchair which is another challenge to accept), finished high school, completed a Business Administration course, successfully held employment for over 25 years, became a wife, became a home owner, picked up drawing again after I became a widow in 2018, became an entrepreneur with my art print on demand business Patters Fine Art Prints & More, and recently a published author for the third time!

Lesson 5 - Always Listen to Mom's Lessons!

I cherish and hold these lessons close to my heart and continue to hear her words in my head. Sadly, Mom is no longer with me in the physical world, but her lessons will always be with me as a reminder that if it wasn't for her, I wouldn't be here!

So always listen to Mom! If you or someone you know is going through the same struggles, I hope my Mom's lessons will be as encouraging for you as they are for me!

Mom's Lessons

- Lesson 1 - Keep Moving!
- Lesson 2 – Repeat and Keep Moving Forward!
- Lesson 3 – Stay Focused and Remember What You Have Accomplished!
- Lesson 4 – Learn Acceptance!
- Lesson 5 - Always Listen to Mom's Lessons!

(Repeat as often as needed!)

Once again...keep moving.

Repeat and keep moving forward

Stay focused and remember what you have accomplished

Learn acceptance and always listen to mom's lessons!

Peace and Love to you all,

Patters and Mom

"Clarity and focus doesn't always come from
God or inspirational quotes.
Usually, it takes your mother
to slap the reality back into you."

Shannon Alder

11

SABRINA LAMBERT

"We never fully die even in what we think of as actual death. We change again and become echoes in others, and they carry us forward."
Eric Overby

Echoes I discovered early in my life that I was definitely my mother's daughter. I had her face, her body shape and definitely her voice. More times than I have fingers and toes, I have been mistaken for my Mom when answering the phone with just, "Hello!"

I thought it funny at first, that our intonation and inflections were indistinguishable, until I overheard Mom once, on the phone speaking to a teacher colleague from the school, where Mom was vice-principal. Her tone, full of authority and credibility, sounded aloof to my teenage ears. Her personality, at that moment, seemed fake and insincere – nothing like the kind, comforting Mom that I knew.

I now better understand how Mom is a very complex person. She was demonstrating her professional persona. I still remember it even more than 50 years later. I feel sad that she had to be a different person from her true self so that she would be seen as valid and worthy of being a leader.

In my own corporate career and even today in my entrepreneurial adventures, I strive to present my most authentic self that best holds all my value, credibility and worth that then creates authority from my own life experience. It takes too much unnecessary work to pretend to be someone other than me.

During my nurture years, Mom was always present as a role model. She believed that to do anything, was to do it to the best of one's ability. Mom's powerful skills as a teacher and administrator were not only evident at her school, but also in her home.

While working full-time, she also managed our home, helped with homework, supported us in extra-curricular activities, and sewed our clothes meticulously from scratch.

Often, at night, we could hear the whir of the sewing machine, pushing the threaded needle through soft fabric. Magically, in the morning, we would try on a new addition to our school wardrobe.

As the oldest, I gradually was given more responsibility in the kitchen and household. First learning how to do dishes, to set and clear a table, and eventually to prepare and cook side dishes and then full meals to help Mom out.

When big enough to work a vacuum and washing machine, I also learned to clean house and do laundry, as well as to sew and embroider. All these skills, that in Mom's house were done her way, were transferable and adjustable as I grew older, to fit my ideals and vision of my own home. Even the sewing skills helped extend our budget for clothes for our growing daughter.

Mom, the oldest of five and the only daughter on a Saskatchewan prairie farm, was the more stoic of my parents. Mom rarely showed her vulnerable emotions to us when doing hard things, like the time the neighbor's son knocked on our backdoor, with his face bleeding. He had an accident with his skidoo and had hit the windshield.

When she opened the door, Mom gasped at the sight of his wet, oozing slashes. She quickly gave us jobs to do; call his parents and get the first aid kit. Mom calmed the boy down and cleaned up his face to reconnoiter the seriousness of his injury.

Looking back, I now understand what an amazing task this was for my Mom, who has fainted throughout her life at the first hint of blood.

Yet despite her stoic manner, Mom did show love all the time in the care and concern that she had for us.

I remember one time she got frustrated with my brother and I squabbling. We sensed that her last nerve was about to fray when she reached for the closest wooden spoon. We lived in a large two-story brick farmhouse and my brother and I ran as fast as we could up the stairs to barricade ourselves in the bathroom. By the time she reached us, we were safely avoiding Mom's spoon punishment behind a locked door.

"Open this door, or you'll get the worst punishment!" she shouted loudly to be heard through the solid wooden door. Unfazed by her stern command, both of us replied, "Uh huh! We're not coming out!" "Unlock this door right now!" "Nope, nah, no way!"

Our repartee through the door continued for a bit. Giggling, we were quite pleased with ourselves for figuring out a way to avoid any disciplinary action for our bratty behavior.

Catching on to the absurdity of being tripped up by an eight and a nine-year-old, while waving a wooden spoon at a locked door, Mom started to laugh too. Assuming it was safe to open the door, we found

Mom rolling on the floor in bursts of laughter. We piled on the floor with her for more giggles, hugs and snuggles.

It wasn't until I was 35, and about to have my daughter, that I got my first realization that Mom had her own human struggles.

Both my parents came to visit and stay during this momentous occasion, the birth of my first child and as it turned out, also my only child. It was not the smoothest birth experience, because my pregnancy caused extremely high blood pressure. I was at a high risk for many complications including mortality. My daughter was born by caesarean section, well and perfect.

When Mom first saw my baby girl in the hospital bassinet, Mom nicknamed her "peanut," a name that has stuck. A few years later, we discussed my feelings about not having another child. Mom commented that if I were ever to get pregnant again, she would not be there for the birth.

Wow, Mom had just exposed her soft underside, showing that the emotional rollercoaster of my daughter's birth had been the most that she could manage.

Mom was not willing to experience that again. This crack in her armour grew as we both got older, and more of her vulnerability leaked out as I matured. I believe that as adults we were able to cultivate more trust to be ourselves with each other.

Today Mom no longer feels she needs to be a role model. I think she realizes that at this point, any of her wisdom for my generation and that of my daughter that could stick, has been stuck.

At 91, she is boldly doing her own thing, sometimes she paints, sometimes she walks the dog, sometimes she reads, and sometimes she keeps up with family and posts on social media.

Mom will continue to echo and ripple first, through the parts of me that have grown to reflect her, in my voice, in my independence, and in my creativity. Then, both Mom and I will get to have echoes in the future because of our glimmers that shine through the woman that my daughter is becoming.

"Gilbert put his arm about them.
'Oh, you mothers!' he said. 'You mothers!
God knew what He was about
when He made you."

L.M. Montgomery

12

ERIN FAIRWEATHER

**"Having the choice to speak her truth or keep the
peace, she chose to speak her truth
and found freedom!"**
D.C Hollins

Tomorrow, I head up to Nanaimo, British Columbia to pick up my
mom at the airport. She's flying back in from a three-week solo trip in
the UK and Ireland. An impressive woman, my mom is a real force
and a shining light.

While my sister got her drive and pragmatism for sure and also ended
up choosing a career in health care – my mom moved out to B.C. on
her own from Ontario to become a nurse at 18. I feel like I'm lucky to
have developed her academic strengths, including a love of learning,
and a certain affinity for the spiritual.

Anyways, mom is coming back from her trip satisfied in her need for
adventure, and half-a-grandma lighter – having spread some of
Grandma Graham's ashes on her family's burial plot after completing

a pilgrimage-esque tour of the homes my Grandma grew up in during the first phase of her life.

It's interesting, my Grandma left her family behind for good, estranging herself and moving to Canada on her own. The family lore around her departure is quite mysterious – word is she was left at the altar by her fiancé, the rumours being that he was gay and couldn't go through with it. It was taboo to talk about growing up, so I never got the full story or heard much about my grandma's life in Northern Ireland until she had already passed.

Grandma Graham worked hard as a typist and sent money home to family while living in Belfast with my Great Grandpa Sam – an angry alcoholic police officer. Grandma Graham also played hard, partying late and living what would be labelled a 'promiscuous' lifestyle.

She fled Northern Ireland and cut off contact with her family during the prime era of the Magdalene Laundries, so who knows what happened there. All that to say, she never ended up making peace with those family members, so I wouldn't initially have thought that she'd want to lay with them for 'eternity' or whatnot... but who knows, maybe at the end of the day, I can trust that she is actually at peace and therefore would be very happy to be spread with her family.

Also, since mom only brought a baggy of her over, and left half back in B.C., we can still technically honour her wishes of a water burial to be with Grandpa. Mom has done what was thought to be impossible: Grandma Graham is in two places at once!

My Grandma Fairweather also has been returned to a body of water. She was a resilient, fun, creative woman. She worked hard at the lumber mill, played hard partying with friend groups, and loved hard – although her life was also not without its trials and difficulties.

I spent years believing my Auntie Vicky had stolen her cardboard box of ashes from my parents' office closet and dumped her uncere-moniously into Cameron Lake on her way back over to Port Alberni... Turns out Grandma Fairweather actually wanted to end up there, so there probably was some ceremony involved after all.

Vicky herself, I'm not sure where she is or how we will be celebrating or memorializing her life, which came to a tragic end a few Februarys ago on Valentine's Day in Mexico. She was brought back here, also cremated, and put in a place of honour in her urn.

However, since then, there has been a major flood from the top floor of her and my uncle's two-storey home through to the garage (Vicky always wanted a bathroom reno), followed later on by a devastating house fire. The firefighters actually went back in for her, and found her urn essentially untouched amongst the destruction (Vicky never actually liked that house).

Completely unrelated(?), Uncle Doug's boat also sank randomly at the marina while unattended – Perhaps Vicky had to enjoy being the life of the party (which she was) one last time, or maybe she wanted to go out in a dramatic fashion. Maybe she was making her presence known, or simply finally getting what she wanted. Vicky has always been a tortured soul, as well as a fierce protector with a massive heart. It comforts me to think of her spirit being finally at peace, and in my corner, in our corner.

Of course, the same sentiment goes for both my grandmothers; may they rest in peace and know true unconditional joy and belonging.

They say trauma is passed down over seven generations, and while both of those women were put through the wringer in their own lives, they started out with quite the 'inheritance' of shit from previous generations in their DNA.

Both of these women were strong matriarchs, hard-working and fun-loving; however, they did not get to live in a world where women could speak their truth, let alone be angry or sad without fear of being hurt, shamed, discredited, or worse. The amount of oppression and gaslighting they experienced, while still remaining spicy, fierce forces of nature full of love and light like my mom... it's impressive.

I'm thirty-seven years old and I struggle trying to learn how to honour my truth and live authentically in a society rampant with the toxicity of the patriarchy, capitalism, and colonialism. I can't imagine the levels of frustration and rage the women in my family (my mom included) must have had to experience, with no real outlet to move it through or bear witness.

We live in a world where there are more and more safe containers and glimmers of awareness for women to share our stories and experiences, to express ourselves honestly and take up the space we deserve, owning our worth.

I'm so grateful and lucky that I still have my mother alive and well in my life, and that we have a caring relationship. I have this soft place to land and turn to for connection and support. Adding in my grandmas, my aunt, and the cleared ancestors I feel are with me day-to-day, I feel more seen from within, and less alone as I start trying to actually live my life authentically.

While I don't believe in God in the Christian sense, I do believe we as humans cannot be arrogant enough to assume that what we can see and comprehend is the extent of what's out there. It warms me and empowers me to think of my maternal ancestors rooting for me from a communal place of love and light; we're all one at the end of the day and I get to carry them with me.

Together with my living female relatives and chosen family, they keep my pilot light burning when I can't, throw fuel on the fire when the message isn't getting through, and stoke it when I need some 'oomph' or enlightenment.

I thank the Mother for her love, light, and all that she provides.

I thank my mother for her love, protection, and guidance,

I thank her mother, my father's mother, and the mothers before them for their love, wisdom, and hardships suffered that have allowed me to land in this world.

I thank your mother, her mother, and her mother's mothers as sources of love, life, and lessons.

"Mothers are only human, you turn it over to God
and then you just wing it."

Jo Ann Mapson

13

LESLIE VERNSEN

"I couldn't see a life lived without her. I couldn't envision a world in which she ceased to exist."
Marisa Renee Lee

Lessons in Mother's Kitchen

I grew up in a house where love was never quiet. It banged pots in the kitchen, slammed car doors in the driveway, and filled up rooms so full it pushed against the windows.

My mother, June, was a woman of loud lessons. She believed in strong coffee, strong opinions, and strong women, not necessarily in that order.

From the moment I could balance on a stool, she set me beside her at the kitchen counter. "This," she said, waving a wooden spoon like a magic wand, "is where life happens, Leslie. Right here. You cook, you feed, you live. Remember that."

At six, I learned how to make cornbread from scratch. At eight, I learned how to spot a lie by watching someone's eyes. At ten, I learned that the world doesn't hand you anything without a fight. Some lessons tasted sweet, chocolate frosting on birthdays, the first ripe strawberries of June.

Others were harder to swallow. Like the nights she came home exhausted from double shifts at the diner, smelling of coffee and broken dreams. Many mornings I found her crying quietly over the kitchen sink, wiping her face with the same towel she used to dry the dishes.

In school, other kids had mothers who came to recitals with perfectly blown-out hair and whispery voices that said things like "good job, sweetie. "My mother came in wearing worn out shoes, covered in flour, clapping louder than anyone. "That's my girl", she'd holler across the gymnasium. I used to shrink under the weight of it. Wishing, stupidly, for someone quieter. More delicate. More "normal."

I didn't understand then what she carried. I didn't know about the dreams she buried to put food on our table, the heartbreak she patched over with stubbornness, the loneliness she swallowed like a bitter pill every night after tucking me into bed.

We fought, of course. God, did we fight. Two storm fronts colliding in the tiny kitchen lightning flashing in our words.

I left home the first chance I got. I had an old Toyota, a scholarship, a head full of half-formed dreams. She hugged me so hard my ribs ached, and whispered, "Don't you dare come back small, Leslie. Grow so big they can't box you in."

At thirty-two, standing in my own kitchen, stirring soup for a daughter of my own, I finally understood what my mother had been trying to teach me all along. Love isn't always tender. Sometimes, it's a roaring thing, a furious, magnificent thing desperate to make sure you live.

When my daughter asked one night, "Mama, who taught you how to cook? "I smiled and said, "Your Grandma June." And in that moment, I swore I could almost hear her laugh big, booming, full of life bouncing off the walls.

If I could thank her now, I wouldn't just thank her for the recipes or the tough advice or the way she cheered even when it embarrassed me. I would thank her for teaching me that survival isn't enough. You have to be the kind of woman who leaves a dent in the world, not because you tried to be perfect but because you refused to be small.

And when my daughter is old enough to understand, I'll tell her the truth. That some lessons come dressed as arguments, that forgiveness tastes sweeter when baked into fresh bread.

And, even though you don't think it is a 'lesson', one day you will find out that it was.

"Mothers are ineffable, their prayers the driving force beneath our wings; their discipline, the magnet for honor—irreplaceable love!"

Henrietta Newton Martin

14

JULIE FAIRHURST

"I wanted to hug my mother but she didn't open herself to let me. So I stayed where I was."
Rita Williams-Garcia

The Night I Lost My Mother

Some losses are so quiet the world doesn't even blink. Others shatter you from the inside out, and no one even knows you're walking around with broken bones no one can see.

I was ten years old the night I lost my mother. She didn't die that night. She lived. But the woman I knew, the mother who laughed, hugged, and sang along with the radio, disappeared forever.

It happened after a night at a club with her two best friends. There was drinking. There was rain. A bad choice made in a fog of poor judgment.

She was the most sober, they decided. She would drive. The car wasn't even hers. The road had no lights. The rain fell like sheets of grief from a sky that already seemed to know.

She never saw the semi-truck parked along the roadside. She side-swiped it. And her best friend, sitting in the front passenger seat, was pulled out of the car and killed instantly, leaving behind three little girls and a husband who would never again hear her laughter in their home.

But we lost someone that night too. We lost our mom. She came home breathing, but she never truly lived again.

After that night, hugs vanished like smoke. Kind words shriveled up and disappeared. Her affection died quietly in the corners of our house. We didn't speak about it. Not once. Except the night she got drunk, really drunk, and the Pastor from our church dropped by unannounced. She sat slumped in a kitchen chair, face wet with tears, and spoke about the accident for the first and last time.

Guilt. Shame. Utter despair spilled out of her like a dam finally breaking. I was just a kid, standing frozen in the hallway, hearing words that no child should ever have to carry in their small chest.

The next morning, it was as if the confession had never happened. The heavy silence returned. She wasn't the same woman anymore. She became grumpy. Harsh. Quick to anger, slow to smile. Especially with my younger brothers.

It was like the sight of us, living, breathing, needing her, only deepened her wounds. Maybe we reminded her too much of everything she had failed to protect. Maybe we were too alive for a woman drowning in her own guilt.

I escaped at fifteen. Packed up my thin dreams and ran toward the first door that would open. It wasn't because I hated her. I never did. I understood, even then, that pain so deep can twist love until it looks like hate.

But I had to save myself. And saving myself meant leaving. My brothers stayed behind. Too young to flee. They lived in the wreckage far longer than they should have.

As I grew into adulthood, I stopped expecting apologies that would never come. I stopped needing explanations that would only tear open old wounds. I understood her the way you can only understand someone once you've survived your own share of heartbreak. Pain doesn't always make you wise. Sometimes it just makes you unreachable.

When I became a mother myself, I tried to do everything differently. I broke the chain of silence with my children. I wasn't perfect, far from it, but I did try. I tried hard to be better and to be different.

Not because I was better than she was. But because I had lived inside the void and I refused to pass it on.

When my mother was seventy, she was diagnosed with lung cancer. By then, our relationship had settled into a distant but respectful truce. I loved her. I just loved her from across a safely built emotional bridge.

Near the end, I found myself sitting alone with her in the hospital room. She slept fitfully, the machines humming lullabies. I sat silently in the corner, not sure if she even knew I was there.

Then, something unexpected happened.

She stirred. Slowly sat up in her bed. Her hands moved gently over the blanket on her lap, smoothing it with small, careful motions. And for the first time in my memory, maybe the first time in decades, she smiled.

A soft, beautiful smile. Not strained. Not bitter. Just... peace.

She didn't say a word. She just smoothed the blanket, smiled at it like she was touching something sacred, and looked somewhere I couldn't see.

I didn't interrupt. I didn't call her name. I just let her be, wrapped in whatever gentle miracle was visiting her soul.

The next morning, she was gone.

That night, I had a dream.

In the dream, she was standing in a field of wildflowers, the sun beaming down on her, her hands gently touching the wildflowers and she was breathing deeply. She wore the same soft smile she had worn in her hospital bed.

And I knew, deep in my bones, that she had found the peace she never could on earth.

"When you are older, you notice the way a mother's bosom holds grief, a body and even love."

Leonie Anderson

PART 2

WOMEN LIKE ME

"Mothers not only navigate through life's challenges but also defy the forces of nature when it comes to protecting and caring for their children."

Sanu Sharma

15

THE WOMEN LIKE ME COMMUNITY
A PLACE TO BELONG, A SPACE TO WRITE, A MOVEMENT TO INSPIRE

If you're not already part of the Women Like Me Community, I invite you to step into a space where women come together to uplift, empower, and share their voices. This is more than just a social network—it's a writing community filled with women who have stories to tell, wisdom to share, and dreams to bring to life.

Here, you'll find connection, encouragement, and inspiration from like-minded women who understand the journey of life, the power of words, and the importance of lifting each other up.

Whether you're a seasoned writer, a first-time author, or someone who simply wants to share your truth, this is a place where your words matter.

Throughout the year, we collaborate on Women Like Me Community books, like the one you are reading now. Every woman in our community is invited to contribute, and there's no cost to participate —just a willingness to share your story and inspire others.

If you've ever dreamed of becoming a published author, this is your chance to take that first step in a supportive and welcoming environment.

More than just a writing group, the Women Like Me Community is a movement. Whether you're a working professional, an entrepreneur, or a stay-at-home mom, you'll find mentors, role models, and friendships that will help you grow—not just as a writer, but as a woman embracing her full potential.

If you've been searching for a place where you can be seen, heard, and valued, this is it.

Your story matters. Your voice matters. You matter.

Don't wait—join us today and start writing the next chapter of your life!

Our group is located on Facebook...

Women Like Me Community – Julie Fairhurst

https://www.facebook.com/groups/879482909307802

"My mother, when she was mad, wouldn't even look you in the eye, as though she had ceased to acknowledge your existence until she had forgiven you."

Lisa Unger

16

THE WOMEN LIKE ME BOOK SERIES

Everyone has a story. And oftentimes, those stories can be powerful things that help us learn and grow.

But for some people, their stories can be a source of pain. They may feel like they can't escape their past or that their story is holding them back from living their best lives.

If you're one of those people, know that you're not alone. And more importantly, know that there is hope. There are ways to turn your personal story into something positive and to find healing from the past.

One way is to share your story with others. This can be incredibly cathartic, and it can also help others who have been through similar experiences. You process your feelings and work through any trauma you may be carrying around.

And finally, don't forget that your story doesn't define you.

- You are more than your history.
- You are more than your pain.

- You are more than your mistakes.
- You are more than your story.
- You are strong, you are brave, and you are enough.

So don't let your story hold you back.

Writing about your past can be very beneficial, both emotionally and psychologically. You can increase your feelings of well-being and even improve your physical health. When you write about your past experiences, you relive them in your mind. This can help you to process difficult or traumatic events, and it can also provide you with some closure.

Additionally, writing about your past can help you better understand yourself and work through any unresolved issues. It can also allow you to see yourself in a new light, which can be both healing and empowering.

In addition to helping you emotionally, writing about your past can also be beneficial physically.

Studies have shown that expressive writing can help to reduce stress, anxiety, and depression. It can also help to improve your immune system function and promote a sense of calm. So, if you're feeling stressed or overwhelmed, consider picking up a pen and starting to write.

We only have one shot at this life, and it's our only shot. There are no do-overs. There are no second chances. So, we better make the most of it.

We only have this moment right here, right now, and it's the only moment that matters.

We are only given so much time on this planet and must spend it wisely.

We only have so much energy and want to spend it on things that bring us joy.

We only have so much love and want to give it to people who appreciate it.

If you're a woman with life experiences, the world wants to hear from you. Visit my website at www.juliefairhurst.com and get in touch. The world will be waiting.

A story is powerful. It can draw you in, take you on a journey, and leave you lasting impressions. That's why I love listening to other people's stories.

Everyone has a story, and I'm always eager to hear a new one.

I want to hear from you. You can reach me by visiting my website and letting me know you're ready to tell your story. The world is waiting to hear what you have to say.

Get in touch today!

Women Like Me Stories www.juliefairhurst.com there you'll find the Author Form to fill out and get started!

"It is history's only duty, Lia thought: ensuring daughters are brighter than their mothers."

Maddie Mortimer

17

MORE FROM WOMEN LIKE ME

Books are available on Amazon or the Women Like Me Stories website www.wlmbookstore.com. If you can't find the book you are looking for, contact me, and I can help.

Or if you would like an autographed copy, please email at julie@ changeyourpath.ca

---

Women Like Me Book Series

This is a collection in which women open their hearts, sharing chapters of their lives to inspire and guide others on their journey through life.

- Women Like Me – A Celebration of Courage and Triumphs
- Women Like Me – Stories of Resilience and Courage
- Women Like Me – A Tribute to the Brave and Wise
- Women Like Me – Breaking Through the Silence

- Women Like Me – From Loss to Living
- Women Like Me – Healing and Acceptance
- Women Like Me – Reclaiming Our Power
- Women Like Me – Whispers of Warriors: Women Who Refused to Stay Broken
- Women Like Me – Embracing the Unseen – The Courage to Surrender
- Women Like Me - Transforming Pain Into Wisdom and Love
- Women Like Me - When Life Breaks You Open - Moments That Change Everything

---

Women Like Me Community Book Series

The community books are a testament to the power of our beautiful members from all around the world. These remarkable women share their thoughts, experiences, and wisdom, creating books of inspiration and guidance for all.

- Women Like Me Community – Messages to My Younger Self
- Women Like Me Community – Sharing Words of Gratitude
- Women Like Me Community – Sharing What We Know to Be True
- Women Like Me Community – Journal for Self-Discovery
- Women Like Me Community – Sharing Life's Important Lessons
- Women Like Me Community – Having Better Relationships

- Women Like Me Community – Honoring the Women in Our Lives
- Women Like Me Community – Letters to Our Future Selves
- Women Like Me Community – The Warrior Within
- Women Like Me Community – Whisper's Within the Power of Women's Intuition
- Women Like Me Community – Dreams That Speak the Power Of Women's Dreams
- Women Like Me Community – Graceful Guidance Treasured Advice and Love From

One Generation to The Next

- Women Like Me Community – Whispers of the Heart True Stories of Love and Wisdom
- Women Like Me Community – Lessons From Mom

Women Like Me in Kenya

100% of the profits go directly to these 26 Kenyan Authors. The Women Like Me Program covers all costs of producing and publishing Kenyan books.

These women are mostly widowed and live in extreme poverty. They use the proceeds to pay school fees so their children can get an education. No school fees mean children cannot go to school. They also purchase food and clothing for their children.

If you would like to support these amazing women in Kenya, please reach out to Julie at julie@changeyour-path.ca

- Women Like Me – Strong Women in Kenya
- Women Like Me – Through the Eyes of Kenyan Women
- Women Like Me – The Children of Kenya

SALES AND PERSONAL GROWTH

Julie Fairhurst offers a wealth of knowledge through her books on achieving success in business and life. With a remarkable 34-year career as an entrepreneur, her expertise spans sales, marketing, promotion, and writing.

At her website you'll find resources, authors, digital course and more.

www.juliefairhurst.com

- The Julie Fairhurst Story – Healing Generations, One Story at a Time
- From Idea to Bestseller – Writing for Self-Help Authors
- Positivity Makes All the Difference
- Powerful Persuasion – Unlocking the Five Key Strategies for Business Success
- Transferring Enthusiasm - The Sales Book for Your Business Growth
- Agent Matchmaker: How to Find Your Real Estate Soulmate"
- Agent Etiquette – 14 Things You Didn't Learn in Real Estate School
- 7 Keys to Success – How to Become a Real Estate Badass
- 30 Days to Real Estate Action – Real Strategies & Real Connections
- Why Agents Quit the Business

"You lose a mother, there's an empty place that can't be filled."

Karen McQuestion

18

JULIE FAIRHURST

EMPOWERING WOMEN THROUGH STORYTELLING AND INFLUENCE

Julie Fairhurst is the visionary **Founder of the Women Like Me Book Program**, a groundbreaking initiative that has empowered over **160 women to become published authors**. With **300+ true-life stories published** and **over 30 books released**, many of which have achieved **#1 Best Seller status**, Julie has created a platform where women can share their voices, inspire others, and leave a lasting legacy.

What sets the **Women Like Me Book Program** apart is its commitment to accessibility and empowerment. Some women in the program are given the opportunity to **become published authors at no cost**, ensuring that every woman, regardless of financial circumstances, has the chance to share her truth with the world.

Beyond publishing, Julie is a **renowned speaker, trainer, and educator** with **34 years of expertise in sales and marketing**. A **Master Persuader** with deep insights into human behavior, she specializes in helping **women entrepreneurs** build **influence, establish authority, and increase**

revenue through powerful storytelling, strategic marketing, and high-impact sales techniques.

Julie's personal journey—marked by **overcoming adversity, loss, and hardship**—has fueled her passion for **mentoring women**, guiding them to **rise above their challenges, own their stories, and embrace their fullest potential**.

Whether through her books, coaching, or speaking engagements, Julie's mission is clear: **to inspire, uplift, and transform lives —one story at a time.**

Connect with Julie...

- Social Media – Julie Fairhurst Women Like Me
- Website – www.juliefairhurst.com
- Email: julie@changeyourpath.ca
- Media Kit – www.juliefairhurst.com

"Our mother loves us. Even when she hurts us. And we love her. Even when we hurt her. Mistakes, regret, repair."

Lisa Gardner

www.ingramcontent.com/pod-product-compliance
Lightning Source LLC
Chambersburg PA
CBHW060806050426
42449CB00008B/1572